How to Write a Love Poem

Your Step By Step Guide to Writing Love Poems

HowExpert with Howard Moore

Copyright HowExpert™
www.HowExpert.com

**For more tips related to this topic, visit
www.HowExpert.com/lovepoem.**

Recommended Resources

- <u>HowExpert.com</u> – Quick 'How To' Guides on All Topics from A to Z by Everyday Experts.
- <u>HowExpert.com/free</u> – Free HowExpert Email Newsletter.
- <u>HowExpert.com/books</u> – HowExpert Books
- <u>HowExpert.com/courses</u> – HowExpert Courses
- <u>HowExpert.com/clothing</u> – HowExpert Clothing
- <u>HowExpert.com/membership</u> – HowExpert Membership Site
- <u>HowExpert.com/affiliates</u> – HowExpert Affiliate Program
- <u>HowExpert.com/writers</u> – Write About Your #1 Passion/Knowledge/Expertise & Become a HowExpert Author.
- <u>HowExpert.com/resources</u> – Additional HowExpert Recommended Resources
- <u>YouTube.com/HowExpert</u> – Subscribe to HowExpert YouTube.
- <u>Instagram.com/HowExpert</u> – Follow HowExpert on Instagram.
- <u>Facebook.com/HowExpert</u> – Follow HowExpert on Facebook.

From the Publisher

Dear HowExpert reader,

HowExpert publishes quick 'how to' guides on all topics from A to Z by everyday experts.

At HowExpert, our mission is to discover, empower, and maximize talents of everyday people to ultimately make a positive impact in the world for all topics from A to Z...one everyday expert at a time!

All of our HowExpert guides are written by everyday people just like you and me who have a passion, knowledge, and expertise for a specific topic.

We take great pride in selecting everyday experts who have a passion, great writing skills, and knowledge about a topic that they love to be able to teach you about the topic you are also passionate about and eager to learn about.

We hope you get a lot of value from our HowExpert guides and it can make a positive impact in your life in some kind of way. All of our readers including you altogether help us continue living our mission of making a positive impact in the world for all spheres of influences from A to Z.

If you enjoyed one of our HowExpert guides, then please take a moment to send us your feedback from wherever you got this book.

Thank you and we wish you all the best in all aspects of life.

Sincerely,

BJ Min
Founder & Publisher of HowExpert
HowExpert.com

PS...If you are also interested in becoming a HowExpert author, then please visit our website at HowExpert.com/writers. Thank you & again, all the best!

Table of Contents

Prologue

My words matter in ways that I do not
traveled to places not permitted to me;
engaged in arguments and moments
not imagined, creatures of pen and paper.

Touching quiet and tender wishes
when thought is the purpose of life,
understandings not clouded by eyes.

I breathe them to life, a song of birth full blown;
rising from the foamy surf of imagination,
creation in six bars, a rest on the seventh.

So this part of me departs into a journey
to the unsuspecting , a visitation of wise words;
always following a light in the eye.
Making gifts, kneeling in celebration of existence,
seeking always for a reflection of rising hope.

By thought and creation, words become deeds,
unfailing measures of a life we choose;
the currency of pretension loses face value,
hidden; it's like what you wear,

beneath your nudity.

Foreword

The method I used in this eBook is to give examples that illustrate ideas about writing poetry. The primary focus is on what writers call love poetry. Love, however, involves many parts of life including love of country, love of children or family, and love of place. It involves aspects beyond romantic love between partners or lovers.

I use many original pieces of poetry, but I have also selected works by some of the great writers of the past who have influenced and inspired me. This is not the usual 'how–to' book in which the reader follows the instructions of the author. At the end of the book, you will not write a *sonnet* worthy of Shakespeare, or a *free verse* epic that would remind readers of Maya Angelou. It is neither a complete coverage of the basics nor a list of all the styles that exist in classic or modern poetry. This eBook is an assembly of ideas that I describe as ***how to love poetry enough to make poetry about love.***

This book teaches how to express deep feelings and inspiration with the words that convey to others what you have seen, experienced, or read. By following this guide, you will discover the way words can raise emotions.

I hope these ideas come through to the reader and that he or she will realize a way to bind feelings to poetry. That is, the true love poem and the main idea I seek to pass on to you in this book. I believe that at some level, one's emotions can connect to one's words in the creation of art.

All the poetry used in the book remains the property of the respective authors, including translations. My special thanks to Mariza G. Góes for the use of her marvelous translations of Lorca and Carlos Drummond de Andrade. It could not be a book about love poetry without the three of them. My thanks to her must also be for the inspiration for most of my poetry presented here, translation of Vinicius de Moraes, and the brilliant insights she has given to me on Brazil, Brazilian literature, Saudade, haiku and form poetry.

The use of all materials presented in this book are for educational and discussion purposes. No copyrights have been intentionally infringed. Full attribution has been given to the authors. There was an effort to transform the cited works into commentary and criticism. Furthermore, much of the quoted material is in the public domain. However, if despite my efforts, I have managed to infringe on any holder's rights, I stand ready to make immediate corrections. My thanks go to all of the authors and translators whose works have been cited or used here, and I hope they do or would agree that the purpose of this book is to learn about and admire their works.

Chapter 1: Capture an Image

A love poem can be thought of as a picture or a scene. It might be a place with people or without, one filled with beautiful sights or have an austere emptiness like a desert or the moon. To some, it might be a place of mystery. When we create an image for the reader, they can focus on that scene and build to the next. The poem then carries the reader's thoughts from image to image.

For most readers, the first sentence or phrase will determine if and how far they read or begin to fade away into other thoughts. If they are not able to capture an image, they mentally tend to drift, the words lose their impact and have no meaning to the reader.

Some useful ideas and ways to approach this are in the teachings of Japanese writing called haiku (pronounced as high-ku) /1. In haiku, the writer uses only what he or she can sense. The writer then describes the images or sensations to the reader. The author also uses as few words as possible.

Example:

washing dishes

sudden summer storm,

lightning...in my bowl 2/

The writer in this example is washing dishes and the flash of a lightning bolt reflects in the dish he is washing. This is a great image for the reader. It is a nice haiku; it is original and memorable. The image is one that can stay with the reader long after he or she reads these few words. Thus, we have also captured lightning in a bowl in the reader's mind.

An opening line can be a great place for a strong image. The reader opens their thoughts into a scene the writer has created, one which begins the process of holding the reader's attention and evoking imagination to create visual thoughts. In the poem *"floor of stars"*, I tried to translate a poem from Spanish to English and misunderstood a line to be a 'floor of stars'. It was my lucky mistake. The line gives the reader a strong and immediate idea of an image of someone dancing on stars. What if the writer wrote this in a casual and offhand way and the writer was writing about wildly impossible feats of dancing across space and time? This idea of incredible acts stuck in my thoughts even though they seemed to be casually done, as if the most ordinary of things.

Floor of Stars

You make casual footsteps
on a floor of stars, an augury
the rhythm of a deep black drum
calls from patient memory.

The dust that rises
inflects the air with movement
as bodies bend and sway
like palms on the shore, so fluent.

A deeper beat follows now
strings sound to return desire
hands circle close
bodies step, spin in fires

the spirits that watch us
kiss our eyes before sleep,
carry us in laughter
and hold us when we weep

now glow within, in common joy we flow
entwine our spirits with ancient echoes.

The opening line, footsteps on a floor of stars will leave an impression with the reader. I thought of dance steps when I wrote it and of real stars. Later, a year or so when I read it again, I thought of lights on a dance floor. An idea like this, a bold stroke, will make most readers pause to consider the mental images from the verses.

A poem from the famous writer, Anais Nin, gives a wonderful example of images. She probably wrote about herself in this short chain of images that represent deep feelings:

Risk

by Anais Nin

And then the day came,
when the risk

to remain tight
in a bud
was more painful
than the risk
it took
to blossom.

This is a short piece, but filled with images. There is a
bud wrapped tight on itself. It hurts to be bound so
closely. Yet, there is pain in the unfolded blossom. It
shows that there is risk even in what some consider
being in a state of safety. The pain of uncertainty is
contrasted with the known sense of discomfort or
keeping a status quo.

A Time, a Place, a Symbol

A sunrise or a morning sky can become a place to join
the day to a deep feeling for a special person. Dawn is
a symbolic time of day because it represents a
spiritual sense of a new beginning. It could remind us
that each day has magnificent possibilities, a chance
for excellence, and an opportunity to exceed every
expectation. In the poem *"Seven fifteen..."*, there is a
romantic realization while gazing into the morning
sky, and an association of a deep feeling about the
self-transposed feelings for another.

Seven Fifteen...

Across sky

time gives birth to day-

a flow of morning light and cloud -

strands and filaments, roses into violets;

on breath-brush of wind,

a moment simply felt

from eyes to dry lips

I am humbled by beauty.

My thoughts float to you-

a moment in your eyes,

a soft word in the air between us;

and I am there on a city street

dry lips and...so humble.

The beauty of the morning humbles the writer. It's full of magnificent colors and shades in the dawn light. It is a moment that many around him might easily ignore with going places, driving cars, busy being preoccupied, or perhaps just habitually inattentive. The feeling of the moment brings a memory of a time with someone special. The writer then compares the woman to the rare beauty of his morning sky.

Comparing a person to something beautiful in nature is a time-honored tradition of poetry and song. As in

England in the 16th Century, poems were songs. This is not an original thought. Shakespearean sonnets exemplify this form.

Sonnet 18

by William Shakespeare

Shall I compare thee to a summer's day?
Thou art more lovely and more temperate:
Rough winds do shake the darling buds of
May,
And summer's lease *hath all too short a*
date:
Sometime too hot the eye of heaven shines,
And often is his gold *complexion dimm'd;*
And every fair from fair sometime
declines,
By chance or nature's changing course
untrimm'd;
But thy eternal summer shall not fade
Nor lose possession of that fair thou
owest;
Nor shall Death brag thou wander'st in his
shade,
When in eternal lines to time thou
growest:
So long as men can breathe or eyes can
see,
So long lives this and this gives life to
thee.

Shall I compare you ...to the sky at dawn?

the moon over water? the scent of night flowers?

morning dew on the petals of a rose?

The possibilities are endless, and the poet

will ask many such questions to connect feelings to an image.

Chapter 2: Bring Words to Life

The poet can create a moment, a place, a world, or even a universe for the reader. Time, convention or reality are not boundaries for readers. Ideas seem to come alive and take on a sense of being real in the reader's thoughts. This includes fantastic things, truly imaginary and unrealistic things. There is part of us that wishes eagerly for the fantastic to be true, and we wish to hold a piece of something magical in our hands. The ways in which we interact with the world in dreams is also an indication of this idea.

Each person learns in different ways, but things that stay in our thoughts are often those that appeal to our sense of fantasy that stretch our limits of what is possible. I have also had the experience of reading cosmology over a period of years- the study of the Universe and the nature of objects in deep space. I have one idea more than any other that whatever we imagine to be impossible seems later to be in existence or can exist elsewhere.

Lately, I have thought it was a planet of diamonds. Stars exist that are made of mostly neutrons with an early immeasurable mass that might bend or distort the fabric of space-time much more than other objects of similar size. I think we have these inner expectations and, therefore, we cannot help at some level to believe in the idea of possibility. Nature seems to teach us all possibilities are indeed possible!

I picked two poems to illustrate the idea of bringing words to life that use engaging imagery for the reader. One has the idea of an ancient tree, and this shows

how much we are like that tree. Life and time shapes
and molds us.

Reason...

Ancient trees bent, shaped by time

turned in sculptor's winded brush

in rains gentle touch or hard pelting

by frigid blasts and icy chisels,

to carve a verse of ages.

Eyes capture so little

yet more than body will endure; like the tree,

I am spirit encased in worldly womb.

Fed by existence- in its many ways-

to reach for all it can know.

Life is a flickered light-and we –

delicate filaments that hold flames.

Our time uncurls until it can stretch no more

snaps back to a place from which we came

and always were; being here and there still,

my roots too are deep in this earth.

When shadows I have made in the sun

gather into an endless night, there will yet

be sunrise in my spirit, green leaves

supple limbs to mimic flowing clouds;

still thirsty tongue tasting rains, and

a place at the feet of passing time--

a most patient teacher-- and a reason

like the ancient tree, to wrestle with the winds.

I bring words to life here where a tree becomes a human mind; a living thing that wonders about its past and future. The tree knows it is mortal and has but a short time to experience all that it can imagine and for which it can wish.

In the second example, the poem *"notes"*, words come to life for the senses in a moment occupied by a swirl of sensations.

Notes

the scent she would wear
still lingers in a wind
floating somewhere in a night
or a dream

and someone
waiting in a place meant for seduction
will find a flower
in the soft hair of an evening
[a lightness in air we can touch]

but I keep the gleam of her eyes,
that way she created me from vacant spaces of life
made me into something
I had not been before

and I am lost in waves
she has made, drifting
between shores, waiting
for the breath that fills a sail

and takes me...

There is sometimes a feeling in poetry as if each
difficult moment has a weight and the sum of the
weighted moments is a burden. This burden is not a
simple sadness because, in poetry, words are often the
measure of how important someone or something is
to us. The author does not write the poetry for
himself. In creating the poetry, the author is not
spending his time on self, but on carving out a space
that only some special one or some precious thing
may ever fill. The poem "*Silence*" is meant to bring

that feeling to the reader and let a measure of the weight of care take on a life in his or her thoughts.

Silence

I left a smile in yesterday

a piece of happiness sown in time

a seed sprung in fertile heart.

I was dragged away by ceaseless waves

into a wait for tomorrow

that makes an ache in darkness.

Deep night when moonbeams begin

an endless journey from sky to eye,

from remembered to wished-for touch;

silent because they too know

the deep glow of beauty,

and the emptiness of lost lights.

Chapter 3: Spoken Words Like Songs – Have Rhythm

Once an image takes shape in the writer's mind, he or she expresses the scene in words. Often the words don't come just as words, but as words in a rhythm. Maybe poetry in the United States has the current influence of Rap Music or the longer term of exposure to commercial-speak. There is definitely a place in our experiences for rhythmic words. The qualities of rhythm and rhyme are inherent in poetry in every language. Rhyme is one of the easier ways to give rhythm and "flow" to words. Rhyme is not always used at the end of a line but in many ways. However, the best way to use rhyme to generate flowing quality to the verses is to use rhyme inside the lines.

Fragment in C-minor

This is the end of a song, one we danced to
a rainy night long, it ran in our minds dreaming in bed
completed a sentence chanced in my head in a visit
with a stranger; of signs that point the way home, the step
away from danger; that mid-utterance moment
that says: I've been here before. In a smile that crosses lips
before an unopened door; a cause
most uncertain yet satisfying to the core. Echoes
in mind's steep valleys, aromas of sweet grass sway
and cool water invites us to stay awhile.

Soak in the sable-d feeling of giving touch, grateful
to return in kind, and kindness, lie full and open
until we hear birdsong and sunrise, once again
and begin to reach for a melody from the moon...

Here, the rhymes are inside of the lines and the
rhyming words give a certain feeling to the verses
when you read these aloud. The rhymes get an
emphasis when you speak them and a sense of
connection when read silently. We tend to pause
slightly in recognition of the rhymes. The voice or sub-
vocalization takes on a certain rhythm from the words
and the words flow in a pattern for us.

"5) Once by the pacific" was inspired by the style
of Robert Frost. The pace, intertwined images, and
voice. He was a remarkable writer with a distinct voice
to his work. When I read a piece by him, I always
know it is him as I recognize the use of a certain voice
and by his use of words.

5) Once by the pacific

I watched dwindling sands

holding on to footprints

as evening tide began

for ebbing waves invite freedom,

ventures near water's edge.

And sets of prints of seeming twosome

crossed barriers, sunset's lowered ledge

by looks of them, two walked close this way

to a certain spot to stop and watch

a different miracle that happens every day;

and by the sight of sand and water

some words of meaning fell, like empty rays

upon retreating surf, and then there were

but one set of markings circling to north

while another

turned inland,

to the sparse grass in hilly folds

rising up to cliffside houses, and

the road to town; water trying to hold

the impressions left by dainty feet

gone uphill, trail gone cold;

while bruising mallet marks repeat

on sand and away pacing tense,

have followed me ever since.

One of my favorite songs is E Chiove (and it rains) performed by Andrea Bocelli. It describes a scene in which the rain takes on a mystical quality. I saw the poem differently. When I translated the poem, I saw Venice with someone unforgettable. The words here have a rhythm. They rhyme in a pattern that I may have invented. The two lines rhyme, and the end lines of each stanza rhyme. This is another element of the rhythm and flow in this piece.

E Chiove...

Float along the canals with me
even on a rainy day, when we
sit close beneath the canopy;
wet and dry, breaths come easily
in moments held to keep.

Falling light, the clouds so still
will leave you long before I will,
into sunset, pouring sweet wine
tasting airy whispers; misted fine
night flowers slowly steep.

Watch the turning colors of sky
to inviting darkness, moonlight eyes
on veranda above glistening glows
stars will make our draping shadows;

until dawn's hazy sleep.

Chapter 4: Be Inspired by Other Artists

There have been poets and poetry written about love since the beginning of mankind's journey on the Earth. Love of country, God, a woman or man–romantic or in other ways, love of a child, love of life, and love of anything in which we find beauty, comfort, or fascination. Writers have placed words in seemingly every possible configuration and yet, they will seem fresh and new when given new voice—or as they say today- new flavor. It is a wonderful way to write a love poem, to find an inspiration in the work of another artist.

Among my favorite poets are Langston Hughes, a distinguished Black American writer, Pablo Neruda of Chile, no discussion of love poetry would be complete without him; and Carlos Drummond de Andrade of Brazil, an amazing writer, brilliant and incisive. He wrote during the modernist movement in a period of censorship and government repression of arts. They have each, in their remarkable ways, inspired me as I will demonstrate in the following works of these artists.

Langston Hughes wrote:

April Rain Song

by Langston Hughes

Let the rain kiss you
Let the rain beat upon your head

with silver liquid drops
Let the rain sing you a lullaby
The rain makes still pools on the sidewalk
The rain makes running pools in the gutter
The rain plays a little sleep song on our roof at night
And I love the rain.

after reading and thinking, being put in a remarkable mood, I wrote:

Calm...

by Howard D. Moore

I give you this night
it is calm like a soft sea
a whispering wind to touch you
it is gentle, like me.

I bring you a memory
a pillow for your sleep, and dawn
will come when I kiss your eyes
and ask for you, sweetly.

I give you these words
they are distant you see
but come ever closer in time
in heart's touch between breaths and murmurs.

I give you this moment,

it is forever like my warmth.
When you reach to place fingertips
on my waiting lips, and the dark river of your eyes
flows into me, I give you this night.
It is calm, like me.

Pablo Neruda is one of the most famous names in poetry. EE Cummings and Arthur Rimbaud would be two other writers whose fame as love poets has similarly expanded over time. Many readers think that Neruda's work has an intrinsic sense of sadness. I think this is partly because we see what we seek to see. There is an objectively intense feeling of longing in many of his works. Perhaps like most of his readers, he sought poetry as an avenue to express something he felt was important but missed in his life.

There are clues in biographies but, for the purposes of this book, I wish to focus on the intensity of the writing and to create this mood for the reader. Longing is a very powerful emotion because it can take over the conscious state and divert thought from many other things.

Excerpts from:

Love

by Pablo Neruda

"Because of you, in gardens of blossoming flowers I ache from the perfumes of spring.

   I have forgotten your face, I no longer remember
your hands;

how did your lips feel on mine?

   Because of you, I love the white statues drowsing in
the parks,

the white statues that have neither voice nor sight.

   I have forgotten your voice, your happy voice; I have
forgotten

your eyes...."

Here, this small excerpt from Neruda's **"Love"** was
included for the repeated phrase "because of you", the
structure of the verses to state something, and then
state the special meaning of it. This poem made a
deep impression on me and no doubt millions of other
readers. As a writer, this is a wonderful thing, like a
new pair of wings and a strong wind. The writer can
experience a new sense of poetic flight.

Here I love you

by Pablo Neruda

Here I love you.
In the dark pines the wind disentangles itself.
The moon glows like phosphorous on the vagrant

waters.
Days, all one kind, go chasing each other.

The snow unfurls in dancing figures.
A silver gull slips down from the west.
Sometimes a sail. High, high stars.
Oh the black cross of a ship.
Alone.

Sometimes I get up early and even my soul is wet.
Far away the sea sounds and resounds.
This is a port.

Here I love you.
Here I love you and the horizon hides you in vain.
I love you still among these cold things.
Sometimes my kisses go on those heavy vessels
that cross the sea towards no arrival.
I see myself forgotten like those old anchors.

The piers sadden when the afternoon moors there.
My life grows tired, hungry to no purpose.
I love what I do not have. You are so far.
My loathing wrestles with the slow twilights.
But night comes and starts to sing to me.

The moon turns its clockwork dream.
The biggest stars look at me with your eyes.
And as I love you, the pines in the wind
want to sing your name with their leaves of wire.

After reading Neruda in this work, "**Here I love
you**", and in several other of his works including
"Love" (the famous "Because of you") and *Puedo
Escribir* (**"Tonight I can write the saddest
lines"**)

33

I wrote this Neruda inspiration:

Never you

It is because of you
that I love the morning mists,
I cannot remember your face
only a soft blur in my thoughts now;
morning mists bring shapes so soft, muted and vague.

I cannot remember the lines in your face,
or the way your lips pouted after I kissed you;
no longer see your small chin
how it seemed to make your face end too soon,
or the way it fit on my shoulder lying close, breathing.
Just a faded memory, it is not you.

It is because of you that I love city streets in the rain.
I cannot remember as I last saw your face,
in front of the old library,
you beneath the stone lions;
they were standing over you
fiercely guarding your back.

I can no longer bring the picture of your eyes,
your wonderful dark eyes, calling to me;
that we could change our directions
like the weather vane on the steeple,
turn south and you to north, to meet and touch
against all winds, and odds, and chances.
This was just a thought on the wind, not you.

It is because of you
that I love the lightning on summer nights,
when the air is full and heavy, alive on my skin.
For I have no more recall of the way you touched me;

how your hands felt like the air after lightning
making my skin ripple beneath your fingertips.

No, I cannot remember at all your lips close to my ear
in whispers of the night to come,
anticipation, light sparks in prelude to your kiss;
or your image, like a reflection passing a glass window,
no none of these things of beauty; all are gone.

They have drifted away, like the boats in the harbor,
to the horizon, gone; falling from the face of the water.
I watch boats come into port, but never the same boats;
never you.

This poem has many faults such as lines that are too
long, too many lines and it somewhat slow to deliver
the reader to the conclusion. I deliberately imitated
"Love" by Pablo Neruda in the "because of you"
refrain. I have been tempted many times to edit it
down to one-page length for publication guidelines. I
have not published it for that reason despite its
selection several times for anthologies. This is also
part of writing a love poem, or any poem: knowing
when a poem is just what you, as the creator, wish it
to be and not revising merely to please an audience or
an editor is also part of writing a love poem, or any
poem. This poem *"Never You"* captures feelings
and ideas I developed from reading Neruda and this is
the essence of inspiration. It may easily seem more
important than the notion of propriety. Sometimes, it
will be, as William Shakespeare wrote in Hamlet:
"...this above all, to thine own self be true...".

Drummond

Carlos Drummond de Andrade was the most famous of the modernism poets of Brazil in a period which began in the early 1920's. He is remembered for his defense of the individual against powers of government and society that would limit freedom. He did not write and publish often on the subject of romantic love, and, when he wrote and published on love, it often had a certain hard edge to the view of that emotion. To him love was a diamond: tough, resilient, capable of enduring harsh and difficult things. However, also like the diamond, it was something that can possess a person in its intrinsic beauty. [Translation below, Translator unknown]

The no-reasons of Love

I love you because I love you

You don't have to be a lover

and not always know how to be one.

I love you because I love you

Love is a status of grace

and it is not payable

Love is given freely

it is sowed in the wind

in the waterfall, in the eclipse

Love runs from dictionaries

and several regulations.

I love you because I don't love

Enough or too much me

Because love is not swapped

nor conjugated nor beloved.

Because love is love for nothing,

happy and strong in itself.

Love is Death's cousin,

and of the death, winner

Even if they kill it (and they kill)

in every moment of love.

Drummond inspired me to write about another aspect
of love.

of all we pretend

This is not a love poem
nor is it without love, it speaks

as if the memory of a star-
woven in the dust that makes us
bold embers that burn
and fill cold darkness

this is not a love poem for we
are born of love, and the fear
of no love, such creatures we
a soul that slipped inside the shell
into an awakening; rebels at grip of time
rejoices in the moments that
race to fall like wind-scattered sands--

the spirit writes a poetry of happiness
etched upon the essence of senses
an unbending will, the boundless place within
defiant of all we pretend--where we only know
to make from loss and emptiness
a greatness of love

Chapter 5: Patriotic Love

The love of country is a form of love in poetry that transcends time.

Leopold Senghor was the first President of his native Senegal. He was an intellectual and an artist and, in my view, a magnificent poet. He wrote about his love for Senegal, his deep emotional ties to its people and to the place. He wrote in the French language. I have read them in French primarily for the rhythm and flow of the words, but there have been some wonderful translations into English where I find a deeper understanding of his words.

There have been many poems about love of country. Most devolve quickly into a chant or worse: a rah-rah rant about national superiority. Senghor's work lends a degree of art and insight that is unusual in any form of poetry and centers it upon love of a place. It makes his work unique in subject as well as in the intensity of its style. Here, in *"Femme Noire"*, he describes his love of culture and place in vivid terms. The words soar to both philosophic and emotional heights.

Black Woman (Femme Noire)

Naked woman, black woman

Clothed with your colour which is life,
with your form which is beauty!

In your shadow I have grown up; the

gentleness of your hands was laid over my eyes.

And now, high up on the sun-baked
pass, at the heart of summer, at the heart of noon,
I come upon you, my Promised Land,
And your beauty strikes me to the heart
like the flash of an eagle.

Naked woman, dark woman

Firm-fleshed ripe fruit, sombre raptures
of black wine, mouth making lyrical my mouth
Savannah stretching to clear horizons,
savannas shuddering beneath the East Wind's
eager caresses

Carved tom-tom, taut tom-tom, muttering
under the Conqueror's fingers

Your solemn contralto voice is the
spiritual song of the Beloved.

Naked woman, dark woman

Oil that no breath ruffles, calm oil on the
athlete's flanks, on the flanks of the Princes of Mali
Gazelle limbed in Paradise, pearls are stars on the
night of your skin

Delights of the mind, the glinting of red
gold against your watered skin

Under the shadow of your hair, my care
is lightened by the neighbouring suns of your eyes.

Naked woman, black woman,

I sing your beauty that passes, the form
that I fix in the Eternal,

Before jealous fate turn you to ashes to
feed the roots of life.

The poem is full of passionate images and expressions
of loving a place as a person. Personifying the country
in such an intimate and profoundly touching way
makes Senghor's work stand out to the reader.
Senghor was the central figure in a movement later
referred to as Negritude or the Negritude Era which
was a poetry movement of political and social
engagement. The poetry comes from a background
when many African nations emerged from European
control. The poetry expressed a connection between
the land and the people as if one might not exist
without the other, as though they were intertwined
spirits. In the original French language, the poetry has
a rhythm and flow that the reader easily adopts when
reading aloud. Some of this survives in this
translation to show a dimension of love between a
man and his country, a leader and his people. It
reveals a philosopher and his view of the world that it
is held together with bonds of love.

When my Country calls...

Nations ask for extreme sacrifice and it is the
greatness of its people that gives an answer. In every
age, nearly every nation that has existed has called
upon its people to make the ultimate sacrifice. A
nation exists to protect life, so when it calls for taking

lives, it should only be for the highest purposes. Today, we wonder if greed and other unworthy causes motivate conflict. There is no such question when war is in defense of a nation, as was the case in World War I. This poem was inspired by a field in Flanders, Belgium. It was a field covered in red flowers, a burial ground for those who served and lost their lives in World War I. The red flowers and white crosses made a mute statement about freedom and love of a country.

Eleven November

From each glory, each day in the sun
comes a tender petal,
beauty reaching for light;

from each lost dream, a whispered wind
touches a rising stalk--
the land breathes now
and the sounds that fill the air
bring rumors of peace.

I sense a rising from the unfeeling earth
that somehow has felt so much of us
our thunders and our tears,
from each glory
a bee finds fruit, a bird calls to the future
and we see the past through new eyes
fresh wonder
at these gifts of flowers...

from each glory.

Chapter 6: To Rhyme or Not to Rhyme

Rhyming is something that we hear each day in music and in commercial words such as advertising songs, jingles, and sound-bytes. In classic poetry, at various times and in various societies, end rhyme was a high art and, for the most part defined poetry. If a poem did not rhyme, it was not poetic or poetry. Today, in the English language, rhyming is just a choice the writer makes. There are a few things I will point out here on the subject:

- Critics associate bad, poor or trite rhymes are associated with childhood nursery rhymes that will effectively destroy an attempt to write a love poem;
- Words chosen because they rhyme rather than for the meaning of the words will also make a love poem ineffective or even laughable. This is especially true of words that have few easy or familiar rhymes;
- Rhyme is an easy thing to do, but a hard thing to do well. It seems to take a lot of effort for most people to say what they mean in good rhyme; and
- There are many kinds of rhyme, e.g., the fully rhyming words like mine and shine, Royal Rhyme, and some are much easier than others (line and grime would be a slant rhyme, i.e., not a true rhyme but sounds close enough for some purposes.)

I have set a short side piece on rhyme in the footnotes, rather than stopping here for a lesson on rhymes. 3/

Some people have a natural talent for rhyming. Many current rap performers illustrate this. They can stand up and begin to speak their thoughts in rhythm and rhyme. It is not a thing of this era only. In the 1920's and 30's scat and bebop used similar kinds of rhythmic words, and poetry was taught as part of a normal school curriculum. For example, my Mother used to create rhymes on the spot. She often performed for charities and fund-raisers doing standup, rhymed poetry tailored to the occasion, the events, and the persons involved. It was remarkable and entertaining. She also could recall and recite her prize-winning poetry from decades before from memory. In an earlier era in the United States, there was a high regard of poetry. People reflected that ideal with perfecting their rhyming talents, and by delivering clever and thoughtful lines of well-made rhymes.

The Truest Turn

Wandered one evening from my front door
off, away from city lights, roamed into night;
where cornfields rose, then faded to forest floor
early autumn broad leaves in full moon white.

First traces of the truest turn of year
on pale limbs bold sunset colors emerge;
over the patient caution of an antlered deer

weepy cicadas sing a lonesome dirge.

Pods, seeds, needles sound steps in driest keys
on maple flyers, acorns, splayed pine cones;
I stand in fall night amidst spring yet to be
on spent days of summer's beautiful bones.

A Golden Morn

To wake with love into a deeper dream
from a place within, where dreams are born.
As lovers weave their hopes in star light streams
to wake with love into a deeper dream,
feel silk of moon, hear taps of silent beams.
Time grants the patient heart a golden morn
to wake with love into a deeper dream
from a place within, where dreams are born.

Hearts can be fragile or strong and stubborn
like glass-spined cactus 'neath a desert Moon.
Where love and passions are as rose and thorn,
hearts can be fragile or strong and stubborn.
A threadbare rhapsody nobly adorns
soft songs that come like winds upon dunes,
hearts can be fragile or strong and stubborn
like glass-spined cactus 'neath a desert Moon.

The poem "***Countee's Song***" was written to honor
the famous Black poet Countee Cullen. He was a
favorite in the generation before me. My mother, for
example, studied him extensively in school. She

recalled many student discussions of his work. The work of leading Black poets was an important source of social interaction. She felt it was a key to attitudes about social change for young, Black women in her generation. I say these things at this time not for the truth of the statements, but merely for the truth as it occurred to one person and it was a snapshot of one person's state of mind and opinion on a subject. This is sometimes the most persuasive evidence of such an elusive thing as social attitudes. There is little doubt that Cullen was influential among African Americans. Here, I have made a rhyme centered around a metaphor.

"when we forget the way to truly sing,
life is a puppet with a broken string...".

The idea being that we have a true self and, if we lose contact with it, we lose something important.

Countee's Song...

When we forget the way to truly sing,
life is a puppet with a broken string.
The hand that weaves the script
comes not to lift us, and so we drift
from scene to scene, without our reach,
shorn of things we'd learn or teach.

When we lose the voice from within
the world ignores empty words that spin:
of our moments that pass, that flash
and burn like match sticks, flame to ash.

For when we give of ourselves to any
such gifts from one to lift the many-
lives we touch, that touch us too-
it is the best that we might do.
Repay the costless hours we spend: to be;
'tween us 'round corner's bend we cannot see.

Life so grand, or for wondrous self, nearly nothing;
hold close as we can, the way our hearts truly sing.

Chapter 7: Images or metaphor

Many enjoy poetry that has hidden meanings, often completely indiscernible, couched in metaphor. It reminds me of the Simon and Garfunkel song *Sounds of Silence*:

Like a circle in a spiral,

like a wheel within a wheel.

Never ending or beginning

on an ever spinning reel 4/

This example is not a metaphor. The words 'like' and 'as' typically are a simile, or a comparison of things that share some quality. A problem for me when I read this kind of poetry is that often there is no metaphor, not in a poetic grammar sense. There is instead a context or a situation in which readers find resemblances to other things then assume they are metaphors. Langston Hughes, one of America's great poets and writers, was a master of placing complex ideas into metaphors that his readers would likely remember. A metaphor can do this with simple phrasing of a complicated idea. An excellent example is his masterpiece "***Dreams***".

Dreams

by Langston Hughes

Hold fast to dreams
For if dreams die
Life is a broken-winged bird
That cannot fly.
Hold fast to dreams
For when dreams go
Life is a barren field
Frozen with snow.

These are classic examples of metaphors. I will quickly define the term so that you can follow the discussion. A *metaphor is a sentence using the verb "to be" that converts one thing into another thing, which in the real world would be impossible.*

In the Hughes poem, he converts "Life" to a "broken wing bird". Later, "Life" is "a barren field" and he extends this to "a barren field covered with snow". These are excellent metaphors with the verb "is". Many find metaphors that are not as clear when they are in the context of a story or a scene. Some are not in any technical or grammatical sense a metaphor. A quick example is the famous Villanelle by Dylan Thomas "Do Not Go Gentle Into That Good Night"

"Do not go gentle into that good night,

Old age should burn and rage at close of day;

Rage, rage against the dying of the light...."

I have seen scores of readers leave comments about this famous poem. They frequently say that there are metaphors in that villanelle but, in strict form, there are none. I think Thomas knew what a metaphor was and chose not to use it. In a form like a villanelle, I have found it becomes difficult to do much with a metaphor whether to extend it or define it. Instead, Thomas used brilliant imagery and asked profound questions.

There is a popular belief that everything is a metaphor for something else, one which I cannot begin to accept. It cancels-out the few instances that a skilled writer might use a metaphor. A well-used metaphor can express in a short set of words what might need many, many pages. Is the "*good night*" a metaphor for death? Perhaps it may be so to many people but not likely in this poem. First, it is not impossible that when we die we no longer see. It is possible that we sink into darkness. A metaphor should be clearly impossible, like life is a "*broken winged bird*." If death were a metaphor then it would be that "*good night*". I think it an unlikely way to see death. Many people claim to find metaphors that do not use the verb "to be" and this too has created a class of things which I call it a presumed metaphor. In grammar, a verb or subject can be understood when it is unstated. I would not argue these sentences with implied subject and predicates can indeed be metaphors.

We are free to do as we will with our language. It grows every day in some unexpected way with usage. I do not mean to be restrictive here because I think in the end it matters very little. It is enough to appreciate that there are definite ways to make a metaphor and that readers may find them where not intended. Either way, whether one makes them or not, there will likely be some who will praise the metaphoric depth! My point is that I think this is a widely misunderstood element in poetry and writing more generally.

Images

I think there is a sense among many editors and writers that a metaphor is a higher calling than images in poetry; that a metaphor is a more artistic style. I think this comes in part from a too-loose idea of what a metaphor is in a poem. There is no scale or measure. The writer is free to use metaphor or imagery as his or her talent might lead them. I write haiku and have spent many hours trying to capture an image in as few as three or four words. For me, there is nothing more desirable about metaphor, although I quickly add that a well-designed metaphor can replace many paragraphs of writing and deliver a message with great impact. I have chosen a short poem translated into English from Spanish written by Octavio Paz. I think this was a difficult poem to translate. I did a good job with the basic feeling delivered in English. Paz connects images like a chain and, in each link of the chain, the image has a different quality. This is a technique I admire and one that serves the poet well.

"a rose drips *morning dew*; *morning-wet* leaves on shoes."

Excerpt from

Listen to Me as One Listens to the Rain

by Octavio Paz

Listen to me as one listens to the rain,
not attentive, not distracted,
light footsteps, thin drizzle,
water that is air, air that is time,
the day is still leaving,
the night has yet to arrive,
figurations of mist
at the turn of the corner,
figurations of time
at the bend in this pause,
listen to me as one listens to the rain,
without listening, hear what I say…"

Uses of Imagery

Words can paint a picture for a reader and leave an
impression that might never go away. For me, there
have been verses that not only stay, but become places
on which I build ideas and values. There is a great
power to words that render images for a reader. Take
as an example a single line from a fantastic writer,
William Carlos Williams:

"It is at the edge of a petal that love waits."

For me, this was a lasting image. One that not only found a home in my thoughts, but became a foundation for many ideas; many ways to express feelings in poetry.

Edge...

there was a scent of bloom
in warm night air, as skies
made turns of clear and cloud

moonlight came bright then seeped away
I chose to stay, there on the cusp
of a sudden storm.

In distance, lightning flashed
thunder murmured; its voice
not clear, indifferent to this dark shawl.

Nectar-dipped brushes painted the wind,
raised to my notice as it touched another sense
small hair on skin and now my vapored thoughts
as if waiting for a bubble to burst
having risen from a depth in me,
the feeling simply remained
within this still flower before dawn

frozen in a moment so beautiful
and so plain,
now a bridge to morning
a pendant dew drop suspended on the edge
of a petal of time.

By Howard D. Moore

originally published under the pen name- "Pete's kid"

Sometimes a poem can make someone see another point of view. Imagery can do this by helping someone see another person's ideas when they might be quite different from their own. Here in the poem **"Small voice"** is a different set of views on manliness, the stereotype of the strong male. Once denied to men of ordinary stature, and then denied to men of unassuming personality, the male image has grown in U.S. culture. The poem moves from brute-strength to strength of character which is a kind of strength that anyone can display, regardless of sex, age, physical attributes and the like. It is more than sex-neutral, it is gender shattering. Yet, there are many who cling to the traditional roles, to the 'he' stronger than 'she'. So, this poem is about that dialogue when she found him to be unmanly.

Small Voice...

My soft voice, you say;

when a roar is expected, too gentle.

I stand in a veiled tense of tenderness

and your eyes judge.

I do not wither 'neath your gaze, did you notice

my eyes at yours; and in drizzling rains,

I still walk empty streets searching

damp city air for my freedom.

And when lightning flashed

those hot summer nights, and heavy air

teased our bare skin; I did not flinch,

but taught you to count to thunder.

When howling hurricanes come to strike down

walls holding the sea, and skies turn in seeming anger

staring down gasping life; when evil crosses

the doorway, in the pitch of darkness

I stand there too,

commanding storms with my whispers,

promising never to leave your side;

standing with my small voice

breath and faith near your ear,

and my ever quiet whispers

close to your heart.

Perhaps this was the end that discussion or the
beginning of a far more meaningful dialogue about
personal strength which depends on nothing except
the size of the will within each individual.

In a Quiet Night...

the spells of silence work well enough
to suspend the roll of time, thought
comes to life as vivid places, voices
blend with sounds I speak to me;

in a quiet night,
the past rehearses a better ending
to notice the start of the next play.
The regrets seem deeper, the joy
more intense, yet expectations fill me

in a quiet night.
Wandering across the world I've made
there is always a destination: horizons,
coming dawn, in sweet moonlight; the steps
take me to love, treasured end of a journey -

and to you, there in a quiet night.

Imagery: The Woman Who Is Not There...

This is a favorite theme for my writing, and for many I think for whom love has been a long search. A long search is a sign of futility to some, but to the poet, it is also the watermark of a heroic soul, a lover of love; a champion of a cause more vital than the ordinary things of life. The woman who is not there, or the man who she wishes for, gets created from the salvage of disappointment.

Night Drive...

watching one thing

as a thousand things pass by

each brings a thought, memory

Ideas sprout like a flower garden of neon

sprinkled by imaginings.

I speak to one not here

joins me when driving

like the empty place next to me

suddenly filled by my wish--for her.

When each neon blade

becomes a grassy swale

combed by fingers of winds;

bright flowers lend a sun dance

send perfumes to fill air.

In a language I invent

one between her 'many' and my 'few'

we travel to a place less important

in time that matters little for anything else

by a touch of her hand to my face

and how I whisper into her palm...

this is the first kiss of the evening

When someone is missed, absent in a physical sense, the poet can fill the absence with thoughts, after all, we spend our entire existence in thought. In a sense, it is the world in which we really exist. All of our experiences from a quiet moment of meditation to falling out of an airplane with a parachute are experienced and repeated in thought, in the endless dialogue from self to self. Love is no different, and the

poet can find a wonderful opportunity to show how
absence is another way of being together—in thought.

Above the Noise

I missed you and the Moon
at the end of a world-soaked day

drenched in wasting minutiae
of other folk's woes, and tired then
I paused when the journey home
seemed unending, and fate
was a giant's hand swatting me fly-like
pushing away a twig in a stream

I missed you and the Moon

as afternoon curled inside evening
even as I pushed the wall of time
begged it to stop the vise to close
and something shoulder tapped my turn
to upward eyes to squint into
pale blue and wispy cotton, wind shredded
canopy that held...a soft golden shoulder
in silhouette upon a bed of blue,
as if to whisper **entre nous** she'd glanced

and then, just you were missed.

So I stood above the noise and crowd
spoke softly, aloud...and told how much.

Imagery also makes the other side of this difficult question. There is more to life than sweetness and light, other ways of seeing any event or encounter and other ways of expressing feelings. Here is an example of the idea of change and whether it is always welcomed. Many people use a way of thinking, a way of speaking that grudgingly accepts even the best of circumstances. It makes for an interesting balance in perspective. Let's see if you agree.

Warning Signs

There were warning signs everywhere

painted passions on a collision course

and time ticking away like a fuse.

High sounding words and reasons

wouldn't warm the bed.

Whispers from empty pillows

made haunting echoes;

and so it began,

sighs and whimpers, sweet tones and subtle touches.

There were warning signs before the eyes

but eyes needed to be open

not half lidded and misted, focused on blank wall;

even bells and whistles

had the qualities of winds and birdsong.

Still there was all of the experience

fore warned by frequent falls,

no fear when we are in an embrace

we think it is a swoon,

loon call on a glassy lake

echoing off the pines.

There were warning signs everywhere,

and still they found goodbye

can be an awful burden in the morning.

Chapter 8: Time and Life Perspective

This is another area that seems obvious yet it bears mention here. It is usually missing from the poetry and song lyrics we would typically hear in the current period of our culture. The perspective of time: 1) that we are what we presently seem to be but are actually far more 2) because of our lives from the past or 3) our experiences to come in the future. When one looks at a woman do you see her as a sixty-year-old slightly bent and grey or do we also see or wonder what she looked like or felt at age sixteen or twenty-five? Perhaps for many, this thought does not occur. Perhaps it occurs only in connection with close relatives such as mothers, sisters, and grandmothers. Or maybe they noticed it in a movie like "Titanic" when we meet the heroine as an older woman, then relive a fabulous romance in the height of her youth and physical beauty.

Photo

My eyes paint a memory
of this woman
lovely face
long dark hair and bright smile
her sleek and angular body
athletic, slender.

She looks over her shoulder
life in wide dark eyes

slight almond color skin in golden embrace
and behind her, a canvas
sunlight upon sky blue ocean.

One day she will be old
and no longer in outer beauty,
sun and sea air will hurt her skin;

but she will look over her shoulder
into time
and remember
when my mouth was dry
and my eyes went soft
at the sight of her.

This poem "*Photo*" takes that perspective. The
inspiration was actually inspired by a photograph of a
friend, a book cover photo—but it was really about
time.

There are encounters between people that hold the
possibility of seduction. For me, it occurs often in
dance, the nature of the meeting, and in the way each
person might be on a search for far more than a
dance.

Time and life perspective can exist on a small scale
because moments can mean a lot to our lives. Some
experiences are typically momentary, short-lived and
unpredictable. Life is full of chance encounters. In
many ways, it is like a dance floor with two people,
perhaps strangers, or simply involved for the time it
takes to dance.

Strangers Dance

Pressed close until we swirl

float in body heat, a give and take

sweetness and warm close breath;

you- imprisoned there in your shell,

me in mine as well- we struggle

as all things must to truly touch.

All the while, I am here and there.

You are in my hands yet lost to thoughts

to moments without me.

 We dance as strangers bound by chords

connected by driving beats, yet this pause

in passage of night rings so true

give all to a moment, give life to a wish

lend spirit to be tied like a string

and broken by a rush of wind, when leaving

One of the more meaningful additions to poetry as an expression of time and perspective came in the translation of this masterpiece by Carlos Drummond de Andrade. Whether it was just the translation or the information I had developed about the writer, this poem had an impact on me. It seemed to be a capsule of time in my life and I expect in many others too; a moment we realize something important to us, a moment of self-realization about our essential self.

Poetry

By Carlos Drummond de Andrade

Translated by Mariza G Goes

I spent one hour thinking of a verse
my pen does not want to write.
Yet, it is here inside
restless, alive.
It is here inside
and does not wish to get out.
But the poetry of this very moment
overflows my whole life.

This is a marvelous translation of a very powerful poem by Drummond It is a capsule of a life in a sense. Of time and timelessness, we can speak of the self this way. We can know little and yet know what matters most is a moment of understanding. That we can have a desire, filled with what we think is vital whether we can express it or not, we can know it, with such amazing insights here from this brilliant man.

Nearby Stars

I missed the last flower
a bold pink blossom, bright
like a face in love with the Sun
beaming in the life-giving beams;
drinking today's warmth from an ancient star.

Missed the last...
was I busy, preoccupied
with thankless details of the day
Did I forget we owe day to precious night
and night to lessons of love?
They have come to us from nearby stars-
in the deep gleam of her care,
the glow of his affection-
and the way they made us flower.

I missed the last blossom of this last season.
I will have to remember it now- forever
precious in the night...

This poem evokes the sense of someone missing from
our lives and the feeling that a hole has been left.
Love that can mean so much that we miss someone in
a way that can be felt. This could be romantic love or
the kind of love we call friendship. When I wrote this,
my focus was on the idea that there were many people
who were missing and my thought was me asking
myself, "Had I missed them? Had I been away, tied up
with so many things, which I could now not

remember, and failed to pay attention to people I cannot now forget."

Chapter 9: How to be: Formed or Free

A Short Discussion of Forms

There are recognized forms of poetry often from much earlier times. Recognized by a loosely formed group of people who study and make pronouncements, but more important by writers who develop and use certain styles or methods. There may be more than fifty (50) widely recognized poetry forms 5/ and I will only touch on a few here that I think have a special connection to love poetry and writing a love poem.

The forms we will discuss here are the Triolet, Sonnet, and Villanelle.

The Triolet is a simple arrangement of eight lines in rhyme. One line is repeated three times, thus the name TRIO-let. The first line becomes important, because it is three of the eight lines. The repeated lines, also called refrains, can add to an effect like the chorus of a popular song, with each repetition, a new meaning or idea. Also, with each repetition there can be a seamless fit and flow of ideas. Each repeated verse not only fitting in logic, but, in a poetic sense, smoothly blended into the arrangement of words. This can be done with sounds, rhyme, and beats per line, the way the words are read in a rhythm with preceding lines.

Saudade e a Lua

she stays-- listens to each and every word
floating upon velvet darkness alone
no wish forgotten no whisper unheard
she stays, listens to each and every word
confused tides of life, loves and passions blurred
An austere splendor, untouched on her throne
she stays, listens to each and every word
floating upon velvet darkness alone

come gleaming into her dark loving eyes
that reach deep in faith to hold her lover's face
the miraculous glows of ebony skies
come gleaming into her dark loving eyes
fragile feelings beneath a thin disguise
search clouds and comet-fall, for one embrace;
come gleaming into her dark loving eyes
that reach deep in faith to hold her lover's face.

Like the Moon that passes ever onward
there is no return to nights gone by
as time and love in an unkind accord
like the Moon that passes ever onward
not one lost drop of want may be restored
where faint mysteries and lost legends fly
like the Moon that passes ever onward
there is no return to nights gone by

by Howard D. Moore, originally published on

AllPoetry.com under the pen name- Pete's kid.

Another Place

When moon made flame upon water

a slow flowing river in the night

my eyes found glows of worthiest stars.

When moon made flame upon water,

came a wistful dance of shimmered light

as if on wings in an arc of flight.

When moon made flame upon water,

a slow flowing river in the night.

In words and rhythms, hearts race like drums;

at petal's edge, a night flower of heat

the sounds of night make background hum

in words and rhythms, hearts race like drums

when tomorrow takes a second seat

to songs of passions, to an inner beat

in words and rhythms, hearts race like drums

at petal's edge, a night flower of heat.

A watch upon the present space, merges

an inner wish to be another place

wants and touches in alternate surges

a watch upon the present space, merges

as present joy and expectation diverges

a Moon rise recalls another distant face

a watch upon the present space, merges

an inner wish to be another place

B. Sonnets

Sonnets are an old form of songs. Verses arranged in a set pattern with a set number of beats per line which come from the syllables and emphasis on them as read or spoken aloud. There are many types of sonnets defined by rhyming patterns and syllable counts, and arrangement of verses. Two major types might be the Shakespearian sonnet and the Italian sonnet. Both have fourteen 14 lines but the patterns differ. The Shakespearian sonnet usually has alternating rhymes, written as 'a-b-a-b' where lines "a" rhymes with a, and lines "b" with b. The end is a pair of rhyming lines called a couplet. The idea is to write in four-line stanzas, to introduce an idea, explain it, and then make a change and in the end lines – a summation. The Italian sonnet has six lines in a group followed by eight in a group. The basic idea is to show something in lines 1-6, then make a change and show something else in lines 7-14. The change is called a *volta* which is Italian for 'change'. Both types are to be written in iambic meter. This is basically like sounding like a metronome:

The WALL of TIME is LONG and COST-ly MADE.

This is iambic pentameter. There was a time when some people in England thought this was the way to write all poetry. The idea spread over time like a viral media on YouTube today! People, and this is usually a scholar who wishes to impress those he thinks of as superior, have added iambic pentameter to nearly every kind of poetry.

My experience in American English is that few speak this way unless reading old English style poetry. I think the scholarly basis for adding iambic meter to anything, other than the few classic forms that originally contained it, is extremely weak and presumptuous or a case of snobbery. In my opinion, it adds little to the beauty or flow. Rather, it does add needless difficulty to writing poetry. I think this helps explain why poetry is less popular today than other media. That and frankly, personally speaking is simply a poorer version of poetry like rock music and Rap. This sonnet, "Sonnet Style" is basically done in iambic pentameter, It resembles old English in word choices and rhythm, done in a classic style.

**Sonnet Style**

In pallid poetry of evening tides

when even seas begin to pause and slow

upon the rolling touch and giving glides

like loving hand, in passion's ardent glow;

in silver splendor of lowering night

finds reflected glory shimmered fair

and moon becomes a bright bold light

'neath every whirl and swirl of softer air,

and there I find stars like a woman's eyes

full of mystery and concealed invitation

and dreams becomes the purpose of the skies

mood magic, captive of yet lovelier creation.

Time defies the rising day and lingers so

moon might wind its dance of love and shadow.

The idea of the English or Shakespearian Sonnet is to build to an end; the couplet that gathers knowledge into a summation. Shakespeare often put a bold flavor on the first line too. Many of his sonnets are remembered by the first line. This sonnet, "***Sonnet Number 39***" deliberately leaves a vacuum in the beginning. It is an apology but it was meant to set a mood. It speaks to the audience and identifies that we are writing here to an ageless consciousness, as if mankind's eternal aspect, the idea of eternity conceptualized in the Gods people have made. We give life to things, e.g., the moon, the dawn, mountains, deserts, oceans so many things and here, it is the eternal night, enlisted in a mission of romance.

Sonnet Number 39

And pray be patient kindly lords of night
forgive the hold we have on setting day
so great the joy in fading rays of light
when blue and darker skies embrace the bay.

As setting sun invades the ebbing tide
a glow descends of changing care and finds
no dreams forgot no loving wish denied
as shining water teases playful minds;

A pale and winsome moon has grown so full
and softly loves her dark and longing eyes
while kissing sands and tides beneath the pull
so softly murmur love to balmy skies.

Oh moon afar come touch her in the night
with whispered wishes and my loving light

The Villanelle

The villanelle is a rhyming poem. It has two end
rhymes. It is written in six sets. Five three-line sets
lead up to the ending set that has four lines. This
Villanelle was written to honor a young poet that I
knew, who died of perhaps the stress of life and talent
as much as anything else. The rhyme is half rhyme or
slant rhyme- "bare" and "hear" are not true rhymes
yet when spoken, I think it works rather well as rhyme
or maybe is just my New Jersey accent.

Last Call...

And now, I think he might whisper,
the hard edges rounded away,
so that every one would hear

in growled stances, his truths laid bare
without pretense or grand display.
And now, I think he might whisper

like summer storms that fill the air,
in a deep and insistent way,
so that every one would hear.

No passing burden, this ideal of care
at times grown sunny, or dark and gray;

and now, I think he might whisper...

Molding his love open without fear,
to hold so boldly, dared to say-
so that every one would hear-

life's not walled, some simply appear
as night to blind us, cloud the day.
And now... I think he might whisper,
so that every one would hear

Chapter 10: Free verse

Free verse became popular in the United States during a time when form poetry became less popular among a wave of writers. In this instance, it began in the early 1920's. The idea was to be less confined by form, repeated lines, rhymes, strict meter beats per line, or even counting syllables per line. This form of poetry raises the ideas in the lines to the highest priority, the words can become more easily read and remembered using internal rhyme—where words rhyme inside the lines and not at the ends. It implies the use of sound effects where the writer repeats word, i.e., sounds, within a line. The main idea is that it does not rhyme and gets a certain flow when read or read aloud by the arrangement of the words.

Free verse is a love poet's little piece of heaven. Expression is the main idea; no consideration of form or style is made more important.

Residue

I watched a tiny spider
red torso, filament for legs
so wispy they were invisible
so he floated across my pad

ghostly red torso, tiny and adroit
traveled over words
I'd scribbled in deepest thought
over exclamations all in a row
next to swirled and joyous B's

around a place where "love" was stained
by a warm cup of tea, a haggard Moon
was left, when I'd blotted wetness away
a bluish crescent residue, a curl

a Rorschach of words meant for you...

as if you gazed over my shoulder;
or you were close enough to hear
a whisper-- tiny like a spider
whose legs could not be seen.

In *"**Next Day's Fire**",* free verse rises in parts, has
inner rhyme in parts, and uneven lines that give
structure to thoughts. Foremost, it tells a story.

Next Day's Fire

I meant to take a photo
you in the park, to bring back
the touch of skin and the Moon

or to have taken it while riding bikes
stopped by the deep flow into the harbor
you in the sunset, watched by me and seagulls
hungry eyes...

I had a plan for a café and a candle
or the way your eyes held so firm
the way they asked deep questions--

had a wish to keep so many
of the ordinary moments,

like kindling for next day's fire.

The shutter snap in my mind
has no pedigree or puffery, it cannot
be transcribed except by workings
of heart and mind, the inner sense;

the precious way I can distill your essence
into a my smile, a warm feeling, as from nothing nor
anyone else... the way I can picture you,
upon winds, within whispers, so simply--
from a desire.

Azir is the name of a woman, not her real name, but
one that reflects how much she meant to the author. It
is a name reminiscent to him of a desert culture where
strong women hold families together. It is in free
verse, a kind of snapshot, a moment in the time of two
lives.

Azir in Winter

within moments that needed nothing more,
moments that could not hold more meaning
there was you, the way a presence filled my time;
kept a promise made between my heart and hopes.

You -- pouring moonlight upon my senses,
perfected by each of its dearest imperfections
they glow and amaze me still--
those moments of you-- loving me

Chapter 11: Special Moments: on Lorca and Carlos Drummond de Andrade

Lorca

He was a Spanish poet whose works were unique and influential. For example, I think he helped inspire a movement in poetry in Brazil in the 1930's; the modernist era which included Carlos Drummond de Andrade. His life was relatively short and ended with his murder. He was executed as a political prisoner and, perhaps, because of his suspected sexual orientation. The tragic circumstance of a visionary artist taken on a truck to a desolate place and murdered by act of a repressive government raised reverence of his memory to even higher levels of attention and adoration than had already grown from his work.

His works were written for the most part in Spanish and his style demonstrated fantastic images, bold use of words and symbols. They have made translation difficult for all but the most talented and artistic translation talents. I happened upon a translation note by such a marvelous talent on the Lorca poem "Si Mis Manos Pudieran Deshojar" which she translated as "if my hands could depetal…"

Excerpt from "Si Mis Manos Pudieran Deshojar…"

"Yo pronuncio tu nombre,
En esta noche oscura,
Y tu nombre me suena
Más lejano que nunca.
Más lejano que todas las estrellas
Y más doliente que la mansa lluvia.

  ...¡¡Si mis dedos pudieran
Deshojar a la luna!!"

[If My Hands Could Defoliate - Si Mis Manos
Pudieran Deshojar ..,
http://www.poemhunter.com/poem/if-my-hands-
could-defoliate-si-mis-manos-pudieran

-deshojar/ (accessed October 31, 2011)].

Excerpt as Translated by Mariza G. Góes

"I pronounce your name,
in this dark night,
and your name sounds
more distant than ever.
More distant that all stars
and more doleful than a calm rain.

  ...If only my fingers could
defoliate the moon!"

This was the concept that Lorca presented, related by
Ms. Goes' note the Moon added to all its beauty, in the
image of a flower in the night sky; the brilliant
moonlight becomes its petals. The translation of
Lorca's poem is similarly excellent, having the magic
and artistry it seems that he intended.

Petalas...

A poem she never read
like the leaf of a tree in autumn
shed the life of summer plenty
to hold the last of the Sun.

Words left to float as if on a wind
to chance her cheek, or that waited
until she was alone in a glow
in the deep kiss of night,

and fell at her feet, in moon petals....

This is a deeply romantic image, the Moon as a flower,
the woman and petals falling near her. The Moon is a
symbol of hope and passion. It is no accident that for
ages of human history, poetry and passion have
centered on a romance with the Moon. So here Lorca
wanted to have the power to "depetal" the Moon,
perhaps to lay a cosmic offering at the feet of his lover.
The inspiration adds the idea of a poem never read.
The stillness created by that line will stay with the
reader, causes the mind to drift to situations like that.
We depend completely on poetry and on the idea that
our words will reach someone. A poem unread is like a
voice in the mountains that makes an echo, but is
never heard by anyone else. It is an image that causes
reflection.

Drummond

In many ways, he is the great Brazilian poet. Although I am expressing my single person point of view. He is my favorite Brazilian poet, and one of my all-time favorite writers. He was a brilliant man. I have read some of his works in Portuguese and English. I have been amazed at his intellect, plus totally taken by his skills as a writer. A major part of this is because I have discovered excellent and artistic English translations that reflected the enormous talent he possessed. Derivative works that embodied the fabulous way Drummond created and maintained imagery in poetry. He took on difficult subjects like political repression, censorship, war and the horrors of combat.

Amar

by Carlos Drummond de Andrade

Que pode uma criatura senão, entre criaturas, amar? amar e esquecer, amar e malamar, amar, desamar, amar? sempre, e até de olhos vidrados, amar? Que pode, pergunto, o ser amoroso, sozinho, em rotação universal, senão rodar também, e amar? amar o que o mar traz à praia, o que ele sepulta, e o que, na brisa marinha, é sal, ou precisão de amor, ou simples ânsia? Amar solenemente as palmas do deserto, o que é entrega ou adoração expectante, e amar o inóspito, o áspero, um vaso sem flor, um chão de ferro, e o peito inerte, e a rua vista em sonho, e uma ave de rapina. Este o nosso destino: amor sem conta, distribuído pelas coisas pérfidas ou nulas, doação ilimitada a uma completa ingratidão, e na concha vazia do amor à procura medrosa, paciente, de mais e mais amor. Amar a nossa falta mesma de amor, e na secura nossa, amar a água implícita, e o beijo tácito, e a sede infinita.

(Carlos Drummond de Andrade)

This has been described to me as a very Brazilian piece of literature. It is difficult, for this reason, to translate because so many attitudes and ways of seeing the world that reflect Brazil's culture here. Read in Portuguese, the repetition of Amar (pronounced A-mach) gives the poem a feeling like a sonnet or a form poem. However, each mention of love has a distinct purpose and meaning. It contains many ways to see and understand this concept of love. The source was impeccable and wise, in my opinion. I consider this translation to be a fragment; a work that I will no doubt revisit and improve in its translation. Yet it pleased me more than any other I had read so it is included here:

Love (Amar)

translated by Howard D. Moore

Amar [to love]

by Carlos Drummond de Andrade

what can such a creature do
among such creatures but love?
love and forget
love and love badly,
love, stop loving, love?
love always- even with glazed eyes?

What else, I wonder, can a loving man do

alone, amidst the rotation of the universe

but rotate with it, and love

love what the sea brings to the beaches

or which she buries, and that the sea breeze is salt

or the precision of love, or a simple desire?

To love solemnly the desert palms,

or what is in a surrender or an awaited adoration;

to love the inhospitable and the unrefined,

a vase without flowers, the depleted soil,
a slow and reluctant heart, the street created in a
dream,

and the bird of prey.

That is our fate: boundless love,
to be shared among indifferent or even silly things
an unlimited gift to the completely ungrateful;
and in the vacant shell of love- the fearful
patient search for more and more love.

To love the very lack of love, in our arid air
to love the implicit water, the tacit kiss, the infinite
thirst.

After reading "Amar" by Drummond in Portuguese,
after parsing the Portuguese into English, I was not
able to focus on the entire work because there were
too many important parts each of which became ideas
for writing. This is the effect of Drummond's work on
me, an onslaught of ideas. He is one of a few authors
in poetry who offer answers to profound questions
that I can find satisfying. It is not that I accept his
views, clearly acceptance is not what he wished. It is
an engagement of ideas. He argues so persuasively,
passionately for his views, that one feels compelled to
engage them. I often get involved with concepts that
are only implied in his ideas. I examine contexts (the
logic framework), looking at aspects of an issue that
often I had not noticed nor articulated beforehand. I
think the reader will agree, engagement is far better
than acceptance and far more useful for individual
growth. Months, perhaps a year later, I wrote the
poem "Inspired by...". It contained memories of the
original work, distilled ideas and yet it felt as if I had

just scratched the surface. This is the power of intellect. It is something that we all use to define the world for understanding. It is the rare person, rarer still in the role of writer, who can communicate that process, and can show to another how he understands the world around him.

Inspired by...

We are creatures of love
held fast in its beauty
and yet we wander
but everywhere it finds us
as a lone desert cactus blossoms for the Moon.

We wander
and love follows us;
we are like treasures pushed upon the shores
once lost to seas and mystery 'til delivered once more.

We learn to love the tides
to see the mirror of eternal deeps in night skies
that bring waves of curled white stars
to tell us that light is forever
and we are ever within the light.

We have the limitless gift of love
tied to a boundless place within us;
It holds more than we can wonder
more than thirst for life can sustain,
but it is first poured upon our shallow palms
and so, we wander

thankless eyes find a way to avoid seeing that
which cannot be hidden
never be forbidden,
never be undone;

we are implicit in love, caressed by its breath,
reflected as nowhere else in its vision;
we are the sullen moon that has only the Sun,
that it needs 'to be', and to be... radiant.

What does life mean to one such as we are;
what must a creature of love do...

it must love.

A note about longing-

There is a view that love poetry is written from
sadness. Some said that about Neruda's work, but an
intense feeling of longing, is not sadness. It is desire, a
passion that is unfulfilled. There is a feeling
expressed and admittedly it sounds somewhat like a
deep sadness that passions may never be fulfilled. A
person is not near; a person may never be near; a
feeling of missing something that might never have
been, but was or is the most desired thing in one's life.
This is the essence of a certain kind of love poem: a
man tells a woman who is not and cannot be near that
he is filled with passion.

canção das estrelas (song of the stars)

(ouvir as estrelas)

listen to the stars

they sing in a windy voice

like sideways rain,

like blown sand on window

listen

to the light of the moon

in stillness near your skin

it tingles my lips

whispers with me ever slightly

upon the softness of your skin

 (Ouvi...)

I have listened...

in the chill of night

when warmth seemed distant

like love made in the afternoon

and the long way home

seemed yet longer, until I could

 listen to the sounds within you

beautiful like star song, warm

even in depths of night

as the Moon, that shares

love of loving, as I do

when I held you then

as I wish to now, deeply

as the endless skies, tenderly

as the sound like a sideways rain

that drifts from the soul of the Sun.

Near but not near enough. So, in this example, a
slightly sensual way to show desire.

**Droplet**

Was it the heat of late August night
made glasses and most of the gathered sweat
in heat, cotton cloth sticks so...

drawn to your lips, a cold glass and my eyes
a droplet fell to a spot in the cleft of your shirt
where envied cloth so pale next to tan
a droplet, unnoticed by you
when I could think of nothing else
glistened in candlelight, catching
a well spent beam of harvest moon glow,
near the window, and your eyes...

I watched the droplet fall into darkness
as I can never recall feeling quite so thirsty,
such a dry feeling upon my tongue.

This poem is a romance of the woman, but it could
have just as easily been written by a woman. It is a
rapture of passion and skin. There is no touching
here, just eyes and thoughts or, more accurately, one
of the most romantic kind of touching of giving one's
attentions completely to another. It is further
demonstrated in this short piece "**flows**" which also
shows the use of repetition in free verse.

**Flows...**

Over your shoulder
near the perfume of your neck
I gaze at the work of your hands

art and words in thought-flows
patterns to script dreams and wishes
over your shoulder,
near the softness of your hair
in warmth of breath,
in electric air between us— I wonder
whether my whispers touch your skin
over your shoulder, so near...

Chapter 12: Sublimation and Fantasy

One of my favorite techniques is to allow something to change from one form into another, from something real into something fantastic, which could not possibly be true. The idea then stands out like a wish we know is impossible but one in which we cannot help but commit belief and faith. By its impossibility, the reader gets a sense of how much I wish for it, how much I as the writer seem to want something. This is a wonderful way to use imagination and imagery. The words can bring images to the reader of amazing things, dreamlike things. Things that perhaps remind us of childhood when we let ourselves be ruled by our imaginations, and everything seemed possible.

A Found Feather

Above the sand

wind and gull cackles blend

sea spray rainbows, prisms in sunbeam glints

I squint into horizon, where sky blue melts

cloudy bands at the edge of the world.

In a taste of salt, memory of sand upon skin

mind lifts my spirit to hover, cupped wings

tilted to catch the solid seams of moving air-

a weightless metapoise: man into bird, wishes

dissolve bird into wind song.

Upon a current stream, a flow of deep desires

carried to a place near your lips,

to make a soft moist rush of air

touch your smile, just while

a feather falls near your feet

to catch your eye, and find ... a memory.

Chapter 13: Some Words and Poetry about Spiritual Love

Humans have the mental ability to create. This is a vast and wonderful power that sadly most of us take for granted. I have had a notion most of my life that this is truly the way in which we are in the image of God, for those who choose not to believe then it would be in the human idea of God. It matters little for the point is we too are creators. William Shakespeare once wrote, Hamlet Act I, scene ii: ... "I could be bounded in a nutshell, and count myself a king of infinite space...". The human mind can create a universe; it can explore the physical one which houses our ideas of reality. Thoughts that probe the very fabric of existence, and aided by the chain of knowledge resulting from generations of scientific creativity.

Endless...

If we could wrap our love
whole around another's soul
hold it for a day,
it would be an endless day,

for there are some
we would never let go,

for some
we would spend the essence of us,
to keep them, to have them stay,

close and cloaked

warm

covered in all that we can give.

Love between father and child is a brilliant opportunity for the poetry of love It is tender, revealing, and involves something very powerful in the way we might project a part of our lives into an unknowable future. There is a point in time beyond our control, beyond our ability to take comfort in an expectation. The lives of our children, our greatest investment, is an open book of blank pages. Many of those pages, we do not expect to see and, in normal flow of events, we will not see them. So, when we engage our children, it is always with the idea that one day we will only be alive in their memories. The things we have done, words, gestures, and the lessons given will travel on without us.

Ripples

Watching my stone across the still waters

counting the skipping steps, following the ripples

rings ever outward 'til touching and on still

looking into the calm wide brown eyes

sweet child and the trusting innocence

asking always why the world seems so indifferent,
hard

swallowing to pause, pausing to gather

thoughts mean so much at this moment

moving from my mind, my spirit to hers

a father's love, ripples on the waters, 'til touching

Chapter 14: A Kind of Saudade

The African experience in the Americas can be divided into some meaningful periods of time: 1) the modern era of independent African nations struggling for economic viability, still a vast reservoir of natural resources and beauty;

2) the neo-colonial era before, after and between the World Wars was characterized by European exploitation of resources and cultures, 3) the early history of the world where Africa gave the fundamentals of culture and science to the rest of the world from parts of Sumerian and Persian Empires, Egypt, Alexander and the Greek Ascendancy, and Rome, and 4) finally, the epoch of 1500's through the present day of the enslavement and subsequent struggle for liberation of African peoples in the Caribbean, North and South Americas.

The experience within this last-mentioned epoch was marked by an extreme difference between South and North America. South America under the influence of the Catholic Church made slavery a transition was painful and costly. It was far less damaging to lives and cultures than the Chattel Slavery system in North America. That system attempted to stamp out culture, and create a permanent subclass of people with the legal status of animals. Rape and murder were legalized when done by owners to slaves. The system was enforced by public laws, mores, and physically by death and violence.

Some of the most passion filled poetry about love has centered on the Diaspora that resulted from the tragic era of slavery. Tragic because of the morality of the thing: a group of greedy men legalized kidnapping, unlawful detention, imprisonment, rape and murder all for the purpose of creating billions of dollars in personal wealth. It is a lesson from then to now of the dangers of giving the private sector power to determine the laws and morality of our societies. Greed has no morality and taking lives, the most horrible thing we can do, is simply a means to an end for a few.

Love across time, love embodied in sacrifice and faith. The struggle for freedom and then to equality has been an adventure seen over and over again in human history. Each repetition has unique attributes, incomparable courage and devotion to a future that for centuries could only be realized in dreams and wishes.

With this background, the reader can imagine the feelings of a free, black man in a thoughtful and reflective moment in an era characterized by the election of a black man as President of the United States, ubiquitous figures of wealth and success like Oprah Winfrey, heroes of a social struggle like Martin Luther King and Malcolm X, and, most important on this case, a personal history traced back to my slave ancestors in the 1800's in America. An occasion like the Fourth of July can become a spiritual moment.

There is love that transcends time and thrives in the spirit's desire to touch the untouchable, a sadness that fills a space equally occupied by gratitude and love of people who have done, what seemed, could not be done and endured what seemed to be unendurable.

Fourth of July

He was such an ordinary god
held a lash of obedience in pale-skinned hands
and in the eyes, a cold cobalt, like the seas
an even more fervent and ordinary god had wrought
passage for freedom.
Now, the test of his purpose, could he
recreate a free man into fodder for his infinite greed.

The lash brought lightning behind squinted eyes
and thunders of pain to the sun kissed child
and I believe --as in the truth of love--
he prayed for me, in that very moment
so many lives before; and I felt the rush of his breath.

Ebony snowflakes in Alabama clay
and I came spilled from amber glow brine
with a caul and a whimper, answer to wishes;
long- called blessing to a line
crossed seas and re-rooted into strong trees.

This night I watch

beneath my silent sky, 'neath bright freedom lights;
and wonder of him and her, the whisperers of my
making,
how to bless a thought that came into a life,
more reverence is needed than I can give.

I celebrate a thing they dreamed, walk
and defy the noisy night with a silent way.
I listen for the rush of a soft wind,
search a drooping fir for hungers
that still cloak air and make it precious; it is

a time to know freedom and...memory of love.

Note: Saudade as used in this Chapter is a uniquely Brazilian word and idea, one taught to me by one of my best teachers of important things about life as well as poetry. It came to mean something when it was explained in the context of a poem about a man who was a slave in Brazil. He remembered his home in Africa although he had come to America as a slave, won freedom, and lived a full life there. He had wished always to see his home in Africa again, but never did. As he aged and approached the end of his life, he knew he would never see the place again. The sense of his sadness was a Saudade but more profound than missing a place was missing the people. A layer beyond that was the knowledge that even if he had returned, the Africa that he knew had been destroyed by the massive violence and theft of lives carried out by Europeans and Americans. It would be difficult today to imagine such a thing as happened then: for so much of a vast continent to be invaded and stripped of peoples and cultures. That was the true nature of this man's realization because he could not go home; home was no longer there. For the unreachable place that had disappeared from the face of the Earth, there was an immense feeling of desire, loss and impossibility. This began to explain to me the concept of Saudade-[thank you once again, Mariza Góes, for a lesson I shall never forget].

Chapter 15: Love that is Timeless and Eternal

The poet sometimes reaches for an expression of love that is consistent with his or her view of existence. We think of love as a creation of life, a unique part of the human experience although I personally feel strongly that many intelligent animals can create bonds of love. The poet sometimes has a view of time as eternal but full of episodes. A lifetime might be such an episode. Many cultures and belief systems hold this idea of the soul as a vehicle for journeys in existence. To a Western way of thinking, the Eastern philosophies seem more abundant in this quality but, in recent decades, there has been a gradual infiltration of Eastern ideas into Western thought.

The New Age movement (or philosophy) was one episode and many prominent Western books and theorists have given recent life to these ideas. One that I read and remember from many years back for this was "***the Seat of the Soul***" 6/ The idea of the spirit self on manifold journeys.

 Here is an example from a brilliant writer, a source of many ageless classics, Rabindranath Tagore.

Unending Love

by Rabindranath Tagore

I seem to have loved you in numberless forms, numberless times...

In life after life, in age after age, forever.
My spellbound heart has made and remade the
necklace of songs,
That you take as a gift, wear round your neck in your
many forms,
In life after life, in age after age, forever.

Whenever I hear old chronicles of love, it's age-old
pain,
It's ancient tale of being apart or together.
As I stare on and on into the past, in the end you
emerge,
Clad in the light of a pole-star piercing the darkness of
time:
You become an image of what is remembered forever.

You and I have floated here on the stream that brings
from the fount.
At the heart of time, love of one for another.
We have played along side millions of lovers, shared
in the same
Shy sweetness of meeting, the same distressful tears
of farewell-
Old love but in shapes that renew and renew forever.

Today it is heaped at your feet, it has found its end in
you
The love of all man's days both past and forever:
Universal joy, universal sorrow, universal life.
The memories of all loves merging with this one love
of ours –
And the songs of every poet past and forever.

Is love an eternal thing? Does it exist and continue
to exist? Does part of us continue to exist forever?
Nature offers many examples of things that persist in

vast amounts of time. We see starlight that has traveled for billions of years. It touches us from a past that we can only even imagine through science. Stars "live" for billions of years conflagrations in the coldest cold of space. The universe is so vast and varied that anything we can imagine seems to be found somewhere in the tiny specks of space that we can detect with instruments or even with our most powerful instrument of discovery: the human imagination.

Thornton Wilder, **The Bridge of San Luis Rey** z /, wrote about the meaning of existence in an examination of the lives of five people who died while crossing a magnificent bridge in the high mountains. It considers questions such as why tragic things happen; and why sometimes to such good people.

Here the focus is on the part of the book that deals with the following:

"But soon we shall die and all memory of those five will have left earth, and we ourselves shall be loved for a while and forgotten. But the love will have been enough; all those impulses of love return to the love that made them. Even memory is not necessary for love. There is a land of the living and a land of the dead and the bridge is love, the only survival, the only meaning."

Love is the bridge between transcendent states of existence and is quite a profound commentary whether one agrees notwithstanding one can be impressed with the magnitude of the suggestion: A creation of human life that extends beyond us in such vital ways.

Again and Again

by Rainier Maria Wilke

Again and again, however we know the landscape of love

and the little churchyard there, with its sorrowing names,

and the frighteningly silent abyss into which the others

fall: again and again the two of us walk out together

under the ancient trees, lie down again and again

among the flowers, face to face with the sky.

In Rilke we have an extraordinarily brilliant man like Drummond de Andrade, he had a dazzling intellect committed to poetry during an age of turmoil. Here Rilke elevates the experience of love above the trappings of mortality. Finding purity in such a spiritual level love- during and after - transcends the end of life. One must remark at the brevity of the poem. Few lines and few words but the experience he speaks of can be felt as a ritual of meditation, a practiced rite of togetherness, fearlessly facing the most fearsome part of life for most with doubtless faith.

Vinicius De Moraes authored a sonnet which stands as a wonderful example of the idea we feature in the chapter, love that transcends time.

Excerpts from

Soneto de Fidelidade

by Vinicius de Moraes

De tudo ao meu amor serei atento
Antes, e com tal zelo, e sempre, e tanto

...

Eu possa me dizer do amor (que tive):

Que não seja imortal, posto que é chama

Mas que seja infinito enquanto dure.

Excerpts from

Sonnet of Fidelity

by Vinicius de Moraes

translation by Mariza G. Góes

Above all, to my love I'll be attentive
First and always, with care and so much
That even when facing the greatest enchantment
By love be more enchanted my thoughts.

....
I'll be able to say to myself of the love (I had):
Be not immortal, since it is flame
But be infinite while it lasts.

Let love "...be infinite while it lasts"

I believe this is a wonderful ideal and so expressive of
a valuable principle. Love can be boundless, giving
without reserve. It is an ideal we could all reach for.
This is a kind of love that can often evade people in
the real world, a love that defies temptation, a belief in
faithfulness that seems vitally important. Most of us
experience both sides of the question in our lives,
among friends and acquaintances, family, and in the
constant presence of this theme in literature,
television programming and movies. A moral choice is
usually by definition a difficult one. But for those who
make choices such as this, to dedicate one's life to
something, perhaps it is the easier way to live, the
happier way, content and in accord with beliefs. I
think that discord with our purposes is a cause of

emotional pain. The poet has a choice to make also. I take the position that it is important never to write or say things I believe to be not true as if they were. There are many who seem to ignore this and perform a sort of inconsistency up to the level of a hypocrisy. I think the reader would easily discern my lack of faith.

Chapter 16: From the Classics

The classics and legends that often form the basis of classics are wonderful material for the poet, and love is a theme that has filled the imaginations of humans since the first words were written. Perhaps the earliest records of civilizations reflect love or honor to an idea of God, or such as an overwhelming importance of nature such as sun, rain, harvests, or the beauty of the night sky. Some legends have become classics, the Egyptian legends and religious beliefs associated with Isis and Osiris, found in the constellations known in the west as Orion and Virgo.

Orfeu

there was broken music

on strangely warm wind

notes that rose unto a fall

and did not rise again

within such tenderness

low soft tones, that became a melody

of giving earth, without will to weep

yet a treasure of life in its keep unwanted

wealth spent on numb ground

life became a slow shadow dance of pairs

and leaving an air of lingering tones

held for the moment of farewell,

tinged from within

love found a crescendo until

parting, and a soft chorus

of night, as woodland whistles

and moonlit calls

Orpheus descended into darkness

where even the light of love

abandoned him, there

lightless places

put breath of his soul

into paused spirit

flowed into depths of feelings

for essence of a woman,

and love gone beyond speech of lips

touch of fingertips; beyond veiled

and sheer disguises of life.

Forever is an endless echo

in which last he whispered, her name.

Vinicius de Moraes wrote a musical version of the legend in English known as **Black Orpheus**. It became a motion picture and it was for me an early exposure to anything of the plastic arts of Brazil, a shame for most U.S. residents to be so close to Brazil and share so little of their remarkable culture.

Jalal ad-din Rumi is included here because in my opinion his works represent a classic form in his time and culture. According to Wikipedia "Rumi's works are written in the <u>New Persian</u> language. A Persian literary renaissance (in the 8th/9th century) <u>8</u>/, his life had importance that transcended his writings the advent of an literary era.

"In your light

I learn how to love. In your beauty,

how to make poems.

You dance inside my chest,

where no one sees you."

Jalal ad-Din Rumi

It inspired an idea for my work:

Orb of night

Soft light finds warming heart,

moon low and touching curve of East,

boldly climbing from shadow of day

great silver circle of coming night;

and words of welcome rise

like wings to stir stillness,

amber ship sailing slowly

nascent night welcomes its pride.

Tenderness in rich moments

and she is the orb of my night

gentle light that fills darkness

and makes even starless skies beautiful,

painting clouds in pale treasures

light and shadow upon world all around

adorns a gilded face of desire

and pale glow becomes her smile.

Lost lyrics of evening songs find

whispered winds, echo so easy

as sweetness sounds upon itself;

'til silence of eyes make answer.

Chapter 17: The Loved Ones in Our Lives

We live and die as humans there is a short menu. We can develop feelings of love especially for those close to us which will last far beyond the time spent together. They become part of us. Feelings that are deep and stay with us for a lifetime have a special meaning to the poet, too. There is love that seems to define us, make up an essential part of the way we see ourselves. For many, it is love of family, love as deep as any romantic love might be, and it can be expressed with similar depth and intensity of emotion.

For some of us, and perhaps, it is the nature of the way we live taking so much for granted. We discover the true depth of feelings only after someone is gone. Perhaps, the occasion of loss is when we take measure of things, in the solemn occasion of realizing a final separation, that there is someone we love and will never see again. I go through these thoughts to describe the way a poet might find these feelings when writing. Certainly, they can be personal, reflect a unique idea felt by the writer. They can be about someone else or about the way people must find acceptance of an inevitable event.

These love poems will give the writer a chance to present experiences nearly everyone can relate to in a deeply personal way. This is one that I wrote sometime removed from a loss, when for reasons I cannot explain, the sense of loss seemed even heavier and more immediate than at the time of the occurrence.

Sister...

The sister whispers now
from veils of distance, come near
and a moment exists
outside of time and place.

So welcome this loved stranger
bringing common time to touch
making the invisible felt and seen.
There is peace in the unspoken words
joy in the silence, and
things known flow as if
the air between.
Wise sister on my shoulder now
stay with me, keep your low tone
winds to fill the slack seasons,
make signs over troubled seas;
reflect your face in a cloud,
and repeat it in a bucket
filled by raindrops.

Whisper sweet sister
of the home in the heart,
and the heart we share.

There are times when words can do little to bring
comfort or even a momentary distraction. Yet, words
and gestures contained in them are all that we can
give. We cannot turn back time, cannot avoid the
inevitable. There is an aspect of love that seems to
come to us repeatedly, somehow each time as a fresh
revelation. That even in moments made raw by loss,
the love we gave to someone does not end. We can
miss them like our next breath if withheld from us,

feel unbearable pain. At some point, we remember how much we loved and that we still do. This poem **"August"** explores that idea, that sense of revelation. It was one of those above described occasions when words, poor as they might have been, were all that I could give to someone.

August

When summer returned alone
shorn of company I'd rather keep
and despite all feeling
the Sun still swept the sky to fall
Moon followed in faithful rise

and August held the front of time

while tears covered a fallen side;
morning was not the welcomed friend
it had been when it kissed your eyes.

But I know that within me
there is the ash of life and you
are there in the ember and the coal
for some reason, some faultless moment
brought so much and yet so little.
For love does not change its face
not by age, nor rise of joy fall
of sadness; it measures us and keeps us
and we will always know its touch.

For you...

life is a burning candle
flickered in a ceaseless wind.
The flame rises and falls
we see it bow and bend. It glows

to leave a wispy smoke
drifted into a thousand winds
as dripped wax counts time
of bodies we borrow from ageless things.

We flutter in a moment of love
rise into stillness, reach for something
none else can see, the reach for existence sake.

Two tiny candles burned low
to inner light and wisped away;
[like so many before and since...]
you made days more precious
we watched you; and yet know

the spark was there, felt and seen
in longer lives and memories
kept within the walls of fond fires.
You, the unforgotten

shadows on the wall that come again
when peace is unquiet, or day is gray
when we hold the moments we've dreamed...
for you.

Chapter 18: Songs in the Key of Love

Love can be sweet, a time of happiness that many cannot find at another place or time, a unique moment for us. Love is a feeling we create. It belongs to us perhaps as nothing else in our lives can be yet truly something we own and can keep forever. Desire and romantic expressions are the essence of love poetry. Here it is combined with a musical setting to give another element to the presentation with sweetness and a flowing rhythm. I imagined this lyric to be sung slowly, softly with a minimal accompaniment of a snare drum and bass, piano playing counterpoint. All of which is only meant to say, that you would hear these words in a sultry style from a man or woman who knows that a song is first and foremost a poem vocalized, harmonic words that should be spoken and understood. Here, there are small, open words that reveal all and hide nothing. Enjoy!

A Slow Dance

Will you dance with me
in an empty room;

A slow, slow dance
all alone, just we two;

Let me take away
the layers of the thankless day;

and get a little lost in your eyes.

In soft light, I ease creases from your brow
and as the dimples of your smile shine now;

I will gently lift the weight you carried
as your care, if I hold you close, they disappear;

your eyes go half closed on my shoulder
and lay your soft breathing near my ear

where each wisp is a whisper
just for me, as we slow dance
just we two
in an empty room.

Love can be expressed by presence and absence. The way we feel happiness when near and the unhappiness of separation. This is a wonderful poetic way of showing how much someone means to us, what an important place they hold in our thoughts. In the poem/lyrics *"without you"*, the song is a story of a day in which so many events bring back the truth that a love affair is over. This is a poignant or touching kind of scene because love does not always end with precision. It might end for one long before the other in a relationship. The one for whom it does not end, might find the world has changed, but that the habits and customs of the relationship have not changed, and bring about constant clash into reality. The poet can make a lot of this. It is easily understood and many readers will relate to it. In comments from women readers, in particular, I have seen a reaction to this poem that suggests it reflects a very appealing and romantic state of mind when a man misses a woman this way. For me, it speaks a truth. I think habits define us and often persist long after the reason for them has vanished.

Without You

what would I do without you?
find new clothes to wear...
change the color of my hair
fill my days with something new
what would I do ... without you?

I think I'd wander the city square
change the scene, get some fresh air

rush home to tell you what I saw there
rush home, ...then I'd remember

_what would I do without you?
I think it would be
all that I could do
to pull down the shades and be
...without you

think I saw you on a subway car
or near a table at our favorite bar
I'd see your eyes in a crowd
I'd stop myself calling out loud

going home at night I'd stop to buy
your favorite flavor, then wonder why
as I passed the flower stand
there'd be a flower in my hand

what would I do without you?
Yes, I think it would be
about all that I could do
to pull down the shades and be
... without you

Music makes a song what it is, the beat, tempo,
selection of instrument for lead or background. A set
of lyrics could be conflicted or enhanced by different
music accompaniments. The blues have become an
invented style for communicating about a lover's
broken heart. The classic blues song is that "she has
done him wrong". The structure of the blues has many
forms but one is a twelve-bar set that repeats. There
might only be three chords and one called a turnaround to signal the repeat of the twelve bars. Blues
musician could immediately begin to play such a set

together knowing only the key or the first chord. I had this in mind when I wrote "***12 bar love***" a 12 bar blues Em -A7- B7- and D7 to turn around.

12 Bar Love...

Seeking soul touch
finding finger places

and sweetest tones

black brings mellow moans
flat and rippling 'neath fingertips

sharps sing
risin' higher and higher

rhapsody for two
never leaves me blue
just so, so satisfied
[repeat]

going deeper now
yes, its rising to my ear
going so much deeper now
whispers so close,
rhythm so near
its all about my baby
thinkin 'bout right now

hits a turnaround sound
sweet suspended key
holdin' the last note

til it just has to be

rhapsody for two
never leaves me blue
lifts me up so high,
and so, so satisfied

Lyrics can be set to fast or slow beats. I have used
ballads and blues but rock lyrics are love poems that
are often quite strong, have some depth, and
resonance to the ideas. Here is a set of rock lyrics
meant to be sung to a beat like the artist who will
always be known to me as "Prince" -- "Delirious".

Pop Lyric

pre-cious like water in the desert
need-ed like air to make a spark
delirious like the smile of an angel
infectious like a kiss in the dark

pre-cious like night holds stars
need-ed like ways you heal my day
delicious like sweet flower nectars
mysterious in a fascinating way

[bridge]
a flower like the rose in the dawn
a dream that comes after I wake
words that whisper on and on
a chance I would always take

[refrain]

you are the moon in my night
the drop of heaven in my soul
you are the stars hanging bright
you are the treasure that I hold

pre-cious like moonlight on the waves
need-ed like the hope of a new dawn
fabulous like the nights you gave
victorious she came, she saw, I'm gone!

pre-cious like a cool jazz beat
need-ed like the love of the sun
blazing like the volcano's heat
amazing the beauty inside of one

[bridge]

a flower like the rose in the dawn
a dream that comes after I wake
words that whisper on and on
a chance I would always take

[refrain- repeat]
you are the moon in my night
the drop of heaven in my soul
you are the stars hanging bright
you are the treasure that I hold

Chapter 19: Love that changes a life

Love of freedom is a powerful force among humanity during the entirety of human history. Freedom is a natural and inalienable right that has been a constant target of force and arbitrary use of power. There is an absolute moral imperative to freedom and its denial comes as a source of agitation that seems unquenchable. It may lie still even seem dormant but seems always to erupt eventually with sometimes devastating impactful results.

excerpts:

Why the Caged Bird Sings

by Maya Angelou

... The free bird thinks of another breeze
and the trade winds soft through the sighing trees
  ...

But a caged bird stands on the grave of dreams
his shadow shouts on a nightmare scream
his wings are clipped and his feet are tied
so he opens his throat to sing

The caged bird sings
with a fearful trill
of things unknown
but longed for still

and his tune is heard
on the distant hill
for the caged bird
sings of freedom.

These excerpts illustrate the love of freedom. It is
more than an ideal, it is something needed for life to
be lived to the fullest. Like water and air, we cannot
survive as ourselves without it. Denied freedom, we
become something we were not meant to be, a bird
becomes a caged bird. This author and this poem have
become singularly entwined with the idea of a struggle
for freedom, both as individuals and as groups. It
comes from love, the human emotion of wanting,
desiring to the point of needing something that is
withheld or denied. Freedom is like breath in this
sense. The spirit seems to perish from the lack of it.

Life can change when we do not expect it, sometimes
love of a lifetime can come late in life rather than
early. Sometimes we change and our concepts of love
evolve as our existence progresses through stages of
realization. For many, myself included, there is an
expectation that at a certain point we are done with
discovering love. We begin to accept that what we
have experienced is all that there is, our great love to
that time must be the great love of our life. Then,
someone enters a life, at this unexpected time, and the
calculus of love becomes revised. What we imagined
did not exist might suddenly be in our hands. In the
poem "Forgetting..." the issue of mortality is raised,
how we can somehow put death out of our thoughts as
we go from day to day, yet we do. One reason that
many of us can is because we have something to live
for, an overarching purpose. It could be work, a
mission in life, a wish to see the world a better place.

Love can be such a purpose, alone or in combination
with all we want from life.

Forgetting...

you came in late hours of the long day
when glare of sun had settled to gentler glow
and cooling skies held light as if to savor
lingering halos on the horizon

you were fresh as the morning I remember
when mists and dew made the world glisten
strong heat and warmth as high arc lingered
when we forget darkness, lose track of folded hours

soft as realization that parts passed by
were greater than curled roads ahead, towards
ends we feel but can never see; and
how love made everything stand still
you came
and once again I forgot the darkness

There are moments when we realize change; in the
seasons of the year for much of the world, autumn is
the time of change. Summer heat and green leaves
make a transition to bare limbs and cold. There, in
life, are stages like the seasons and autumn a time to
shed the high green of summer. Autumn, in nature, is
the time of planting, for people it appears to be the
harvest and the end, but the fruits and seeds of the
growing seasons become planted in fall by nature,
preparing for a new cycle. It is subtler than harvest
but just as meaningful. In this poem, the

*"**Interpretation of Autumn**"* I borrow an idea from Carlos Drummond de Andrade (he wrote *"**an Interpretation of September**"*) and give a new meaning to the season of change.

Interpretation of Autumn

We have come to autumn
in our halves of the world
and find the way --like city streets--
cluttered in windswept husks of summer,
residues of lusher days.

We watch windows of a year slide down
from risen heat and needs to cool
to subtle freshness of later dawn, early dusk
into night's deeper tones of change.

We have winnowed time, bathed in thoughts
that ought be patient like the stars;
yes, the way, still littered among signs of chill.
We are in dried dust of spent spring,
as summer-night thunders fade to whispers.
They have now become ragged drags,
blown gold, ruby flecked rustles.
Lost traces of us have come to autumn; here
without regret for time I have loved you...

I pause and reflect upon seeds that fall
and covered ground that keeps them.
They do not regret their moments in the Sun;
and I know, the fires of the Sun
have also been sown...within me.

Some occasions in life bring a surprising result, and this poem describes such a moment of a life when the facts one assumes about life and love, suddenly are shown to be so very wrong. One might try to control events and succeed in some part, but controlling the feelings can be another matter. It proves to be far more difficult than it might appear. At various stages or times in a lifetime, we might decide we are done with love and romance. We might try to focus on other things or simply learn to behave with a practiced coldness. Love can be like a force of nature, irrepressible, uncontrolled by human effort. In the poem *"Sweet Someone"* a man finds love can rise like a flood and be just as impossible to control.

Sweet someone [revision]

I'd truly meant to bar the door
put love to rest in peaceful memory,
life gone by yet going on;

answered knocking sounds
so many eyes set on falling,
bone deep coldness survived
spring fogs and summer hazes.

Courage came
in frail disguise
wispy wanting winds
lifting fond feelings,
like swirling pieces of autumn;

distance diminished

edges sounded softer,
so unexpected yet
welcomed warming.

Walls sagged to fall
now unguarded, garden
buds upon swollen stems
began blooming,
folded flowers to open;
softness
sent splendor,

honeyed eyes
dripping dewy morning.

I'd truly meant to close the door
lock keys even from me;
love found its way, like dreamy sleep
to seep into night; forming
filling an empty place.

*La vita ha avuta sempre una canzone,
ora dolce che qualcuno
ha parole scritte.*

(Life always had a song,
now sweet someone
has written words.)

Chapter 20: A Love of Life

A mother is the parent of an AIDS infected child, a child who is a grown up to the rest of the world. To a more cynical part of the world, he is a victim of sinfulness. In this respect, I cannot fathom the lack of compassion particularly by people who follow the teachings of One who believed so deeply in the power of love.

Unrelenting...

There is a sound in the human spirit

rises like laughter- rolled bird sounds,

busy at life - eating, mating building for sunset,

resting for sunrise

 a sound like waves on shore etching caves in cliffs

and laughter inside the cliffs

swallows sounds of the world,

molds them into cavern echoes

a sound like a tear... a roar in the throat of night

hurricane howl, ripping apart the world we have made

from the way we build towards sunset

the dreams we lay like bricks

to remake the day to come

from even the most bitter yesterday; it is

a deafening blinding hiss and cry...like a tear

falls from Mother's eye

watching the soul of her soul wither

child of love now fallen victim to the ways we love

So many ways to love, so easy to breathe

so easy to stop breathing

so delicate this flame as life

flickered heartbeat

moving to the sounds, drumbeat

of living, and the unforgiving work of time-

crests and falls, joy and pain, unrelenting.

I wrote this poem *"Coda"* just hours before a medical procedure. At the time, my Living Will prohibited resuscitation and any means for revival. There was a risk associated with the procedure, a distinct family history. All of these factors combined to give a somber moment to consider what I might say if these were the last words I'd write. One would hope for the secret to happiness or eternal life but sadly, all I could muster was a kind of way to say: I love my life, it is a precious thing.

Coda

Let the last note be most sweet
the song ends with a glow like
sunset, beauty glides into night

light goes to another side
a world still dark finds rising hope
and love is the fire of the star.

Let the ending sound dwell on air
as if it might never leave.
For in lives touched, even for moments shared,
comes the beauty of rising night.

New birth in ashes of a day
consumed before we would have it done
but savored, as a most precious pearl

adorning the ebony skin of the skies
and reflecting warmth that once had been.

"As time goes by", a classic song, one I'd not appreciated so much until I heard it sung by an old Cuban singer, near the end of his life and career. Ibrahim Ferrer, a man who had perhaps been denied a worldwide audience by political circumstances. When he crooned the song in Spanish, the words took on a new meaning for me. I could feel the sense of how precious the opportunity was for him to finally be heard by the wider world.

Qui el tiempo va...

I have a tragic love affair with life

it is bound to end in heartbreak

no matter how hard we hold

like thunder and flash in the passionate night

the fold of waves upon an eager, hungry shore

it will nonetheless eventually be...alone

the quiet drum

without the hand that makes it thrill the air

I will live in this way

to make it miss me,

when I am gone.

Chapter 21: Summing It All Up

There is poetry in each of us. Poetry that we see in the words of others, in aspects of the world around us such as sunsets, moonlight on water, a sudden rainbow, or in a word from someone who cares for us. We can see it in the man or woman we love, and in the men and women who love us such as family, friends, people we make into special relationships. When we can connect our feelings to poetry, the experience of each moment gains an added potential with giving or receiving a thing of beauty. Poetry can enhance every experience.

This eBook seeks to speak softly yet be remembered. I expect that one or more instances here, examples and especially the works of the great poets will stay in the eyes of the reader. I hope many readers will try to put some of these ideas into action in their writing.

Perhaps they might create a poem that reflects something of their inner spirit, something from the essence of the writer's values.

Of The Rivers...

Near whispers of Angels

words they've used to mend my heart

come like a song of truths to realize

a moment meant for keeping

Floating away now,

as if adrift from land

taken by rivers beneath the sea,

yet the compass in my spirit

does not relinquish its home

A water drop remembers

it is of the rivers, the rivers

bend but know

there is one place to end and begin.

Soft words yet reveal a hard purpose

and you, are winds...lifted to clouds

a breeze after the rains, and breath

remembered in my skin.

Epilogue

Hopefully, we all have someone who makes poetry in our lives, in a world of smiles and beauty, one who touches us in an unforgettable way. This is a love poem I wrote to the woman I love -- enjoy!

Sussoros (Whispers)

In my dream

I press ear to the Sun

listen to sounds like wind-blown rains,

the heart's rains;

and I learn in the painless burn

that even great things.... whisper.

Unfolded from sleep,

my visitation to other visions,

I speak to you,

wherever you may be;

in the greatness of creation, in the pour

flows a part greater than the sum of me;

I whisper... Love,

eu sussoro...meu Amor

About the Expert

Howard D. Moore is a Government Relations Consultant and writer. He was educated at Howard University and the Georgetown University School of Law. His career has included work in the U.S. Government (the U.S. Congress, the Executive Office of the President, Office of Management and Budget, and several Federal Departments). He has worked in Government Relations in the Railroad and Construction industries, an attorney, and a consultant to government and industry.

He has written poetry of many kinds. He has published his work in several anthologies and online magazines, and one volume of love poetry.

HowExpert publishes quick 'how to' guides on all topics from A to Z by everyday experts. Visit HowExpert.com to learn more.

Recommended Resources

- HowExpert.com – Quick 'How To' Guides on All Topics from A to Z by Everyday Experts.
- HowExpert.com/free – Free HowExpert Email Newsletter.
- HowExpert.com/books – HowExpert Books
- HowExpert.com/courses – HowExpert Courses
- HowExpert.com/clothing – HowExpert Clothing
- HowExpert.com/membership – HowExpert Membership Site
- HowExpert.com/affiliates – HowExpert Affiliate Program
- HowExpert.com/writers – Write About Your #1 Passion/Knowledge/Expertise & Become a HowExpert Author.
- HowExpert.com/resources – Additional HowExpert Recommended Resources
- YouTube.com/HowExpert – Subscribe to HowExpert YouTube.
- Instagram.com/HowExpert – Follow HowExpert on Instagram.
- Facebook.com/HowExpert – Follow HowExpert on Facebook.

Made in United States
North Haven, CT
30 June 2022